$7

OLD SHEFFIELD PLATE

John Bedford &
Derek Austin

WALKER AND COMPANY
NEW YORK

Library of Congress Catalog Card Number: LC67–23843

First published in the United States of America in 1967 by Walker and Company, a division of Publications Development Corporation.

Printed in Hong Kong

Contents

Introduction

The collector of Sheffield Plate takes his pleasure almost as much from fine workmanship as from beauty of form and decoration. The old craftsmen were competing with the silversmiths, and their creations had to have all the attributes of silver itself. Thus the art and skill of the plater gave to his work a particular and unique quality which is scarcely to be found in silver itself.

For this reason the connoisseur is attracted far more by the individual merit of a piece than by its age or its attribution to a particular factory. The fine texture of metal given by rolling, flat hammering and other hand work, the delicacy of mountings, the fineness of wirework and cutting, the neatness of soldering, all played their part in the process.

The fused plater, like the glassblower and the fine potter, was born rather than made; and it is perhaps not surprising that when electro-plating took over, few of the older firms joined the new industry. The craft lingered, but in the end it became a victim of the Industrial Revolution.

With the exceptions stated in the captions, all the pieces illustrated here are from the collection of the Victoria and Albert Museum, London, to the staff of which the authors, as always, have to express their grateful thanks.

1. The Makers

What *is* Old Sheffield Plate, and why is it so called? The question is indeed worth asking today. Collectors highly knowledgeable about other matters, for example glass and china, can find themselves at a loss here. Sheffield Plate is not 'plate' in the sense used by connoisseurs and dealers, nor was all of it made in Sheffield; nor in fact does it include those very plentiful wares you see in the antique shops which have the word 'Sheffield' stamped on them—which are actually Britannia ware.

Craftsmen working in precious metals like silver and gold have always sought, or been obliged, to make that precious little go a long way. They have partly gilded silver with gold leaf, to make articles of 'parcel' gilt; they have also 'plated' baser metals like iron and copper with thin skins of gold or silver. The Spaniards adopted the word 'plate' (Latin— *plattus*) as their term for silver; and when vessels were made up from sheets of solid gold or silver, these wares became known as silver or gold 'plate'—and are still so described in books and auctioneers' catalogues today. The economical craftsman, in covering a piece of base metal with a skin of silver or gold, 'plated' it: that is to say, he laid over it a 'plate' of the precious metal.

In ancient and medieval times, this 'plating' had been carried out by grafting on to an already made-up piece thin slivers of the precious metal, and then so beating and burnishing it down that it looked exactly as if the piece was actually made of it.

In the reign of James I the Sheffield Cutlers laid down regulations about the use of gold and silver on knives. They had evidently by this time found an efficient and lasting method of coating iron and steel with silver, and although in

5

later reigns Acts of Parliament prohibited the silvering of any articles but, for example, knights' spurs and wearing apparel, the practice still went on. They seem to have been using a form of the process we now know as close-plating, whereby silver foil was soldered on to a finished article using tin as a flux.

The process was at that time, and for many years afterwards, used for knives, cutting blades and handles of snuffers, for steel buckles and a later adaptation by the cutlers to cover the steel blades of knives. Its revival by Sir Edward Thomason of Birmingham in 1810 seems to have had some success, but was fairly short lived. One serious disadvantage it had was that if the piece was subjected to strong heat, the coating might melt; while if it lived in continual damp, the base metal could rust and the skin peel off.

We now come to the process of making what is known as Old Sheffield or 'fused' Plate. Every trade has its legends, and Old Sheffield Plate does not fail us. The *Derby Mercury* seems to have set it going. In its issue for 17 September 1788 appears the following: 'On Thursday se'night died at Whitely Wood, near Sheffield, Mr Thomas Boulsover aged eighty-four. This gentleman was the first inventor of Plated Metal: which like many other curious arts was discovered by accident. About the year 1750 (at which time he kept a Cutler's shop at Sheffield) Mr Boulsover was employed to repair a knife haft which was composed of silver and copper; and having effected the job, the cementing of the two metals immediately struck him with the practicability of manufacturing plated articles, and he presently commenced a manufacture of plated snuff boxes and buttons. Consequently from Mr Boulsover's accidental acquirement, the beneficial and extensive trade of plated goods had its origin. He has been justly esteemed one of the most ingenious mechanics that Sheffield can boast.'

Boulsover had apparently applied with his blowpipe rather more heat than he had actually needed to melt the silver haft and had also melted the copper. The result was that the two metals had fused together so firmly that it was impossible to part them. So far, so good. This trick could have been carried out at any time since mankind began to work silver and copper; you could do it yourself today if you wished. But, according to an elaboration of the legend, Boulsover then discovered—either by another accident or by experiment—that the two joined metals when put through a rolling mill expanded in unison: they behaved, in other words, as though they were one metal. Although the surface area was increased many times the proportionate thicknesses of copper and silver remained the same.

Boulsover was accordingly 'struck'—as one commentator has described it—with the high significance of this fact. Until that moment, as we have seen, if you wanted to coat an article of base metal with a more precious metal you had first to make the article up into its finished shape, then solder on to it in some way a thin sheet of the required coating. This could be extremely costly in labour and materials and, as already noted, was not at all as durable as it might be. But Boulsover's discovery suggested that it might be possible, and much more convenient and economical, to create a sheet of base metal covered with a skin of precious metal, inseparably fused together, and then work it up into the required shape exactly as though it were a single metal.

So Boulsover started to use his discovery in the making of small boxes and buttons—a lucrative trade then, for metal buttons were worn by everyone, servants especially using a great many on their liveries; while boxes of all kinds were wanted for snuff, patches, tobacco and all manner of things.

Saucepan by Joseph Hancock.

Sauce tureen 1785. Very like the work of R. & S. Hennell.

Boulsover went on to make a highly successful career for himself, but not, eventually, in the making of articles in his fused plate. By 1769 he had found it more profitable to make saws and other edge tools, leaving it to others to develop his invention—if indeed fused plate was invented in the way the legend suggests.

At all events the Sheffield men were not slow in taking up the new process. They took an ingot of copper—which they found most suitable if it were alloyed slightly with zinc and lead—of such a size and thickness that it would roll out to the dimensions of the sheet eventually required. Its surface (or both surfaces when double-plating came in) was then planed smooth and solid, and all imperfections filed and scraped away. Then a sheet of silver, differing in gauge according to the thickness of coating required, was cut to nearly the same size as the copper ingot, and smoothed and cleaned in the same way. The two were then tightly pressed together so as to exclude all air, thus firmly 'bedding' them into each other.

The older method of doing this was for one man to hold a piece of iron of 20 lb weight over the combined block while another struck it with a heavy hammer: later this process was carried out hydraulically. Then a copper plate, dressed with chalk and water to prevent it sticking, was placed above the silver plate to protect it from the fire: with double plating another copper plate would be placed outside the

8

the second leaf of silver. All three (or five) pieces of metal were now bound up tightly into a 'sandwich' with iron wire, the exposed edges dressed with borax in solution, and the whole placed in a furnace heated by coke. There was a peephole in the furnace, through which the 'sandwich' was carefully watched until the silver in it began to 'weep', i.e. to melt and trickle down the sides. Silver melts at a lower temperature (960°C) than does copper (1083°C), so this 'weeping' was an indication that fusion was taking place.

The fused ingot was then allowed to cool, after which it was thoroughly cleaned by dipping it into various acids, scouring it with sand and water, etc. If any imperfections appeared, they could be cut out at this stage. The ingot was then taken to the rolling mills, reheated and rolled out to the requisite size.

Outstanding among the Sheffield manufacturers who came early into the field of fused plate was Joseph Hancock, another cutler who shared Boulsover's attic workshop. He has been described as 'the Father of silver plated manufacture' and is perhaps a good deal more entitled to this distinction than Boulsover. He was born about the year 1711 and apparently admitted to the Freedom of the Sheffield Cutlers' Company in the 1730s, becoming Master Cutler in 1763–4. Charles Dixon claims that he started making plated articles about the year 1751, among his first

Two Argyles c. 1790, one in the form of a teapot, the other of a posset pot.

9

Two sauce boats c. 1770, after silver designs of (a) 1760 and (b) 1720–30.

(a)   (b)

items being saucepans 'plated inside'. One of these is in the Victoria & Albert Museum (see p. 7): the plate has been beaten out by hand, and the slight cracks occurring in the metal during the raising have been soldered up with silver. Although plated on only one side—the inside—the silver is of unusual thickness. The handle socket, riveted to the body, bears the mark: JOSH HANCOCK SHEFFIELD.

Other articles claimed as having been made by Hancock in these early days are plated spoons and forks, put together in two parts and filled with solder. In these early forks the two sections were stamped longitudinally, filled with lead and tin, then soldered together, the seams being slightly visible. Silver points were attached by soldering. But apparently Hancock was also concerned in the making of 'great variety of articles, such as tea-urns, coffee pots, saucepans, tankards, cups, candlesticks'. Like many another manufacturer, he eventually decided to leave to others the hurly-burly of producing and selling finished goods, for about 1762–5 we find him the owner of mills for rolling out the plate, from which he is said to have made a large fortune.

Among the other manufacturers who came early into the plating enterprise was Thomas Law, another Master of the Sheffield Cutlers, whose successors in business registered the mark of a vase. Another firm which must have been in a considerable way of business from the 1760s onwards was that of Tudor and Leader. Thomas Leader, an Essex man, who had served his apprenticeship as a silversmith in London, set up in partnership with Henry Tudor, of a Welshpool family, and, backed by a local figure named Dr

Sherburn, they forged ahead very rapidly. Other distinguished names from these early days were the brothers Jacob and Samuel Roberts, Thomas Bradbury—a firm which lasted until well into the twentieth century—Winter, Parsons and Co., Ashforth Ellis and Co., Matthew Fenton and Co.

Of them all perhaps the most outstanding single figure was Samuel Roberts, son of the Samuel Roberts mentioned above. Born in 1763, and apprenticed to Thomas Law, Roberts was to live on until halfway through the next century, and see not only every major development in the plating industry—to which he himself made several contributions of the greatest importance—but also its final defeat at the hands of the electro-platers. He was not only a good business man, but a brilliant and original designer—his work is to be seen in his firm's catalogues—and also a considerable inventor. His partner, George Cadman, was 'the first that ever put silver edges on plated goods', an innovation which the firm pushed very hard. They were also the first to bring into practical use the process of 'rubbing in' silver shields (see p. 29). Roberts himself was the author of many patents, and brought in stamped silver feet, handles and mounts, and also bright engraving on mounts and borders. For about twenty-five years after 1785, according to Frederick Bradbury (in his *History of Old Sheffield Plate*), he was the main influence behind most of the innovations in design: his competitors, it was said, awaited each of his productions before deciding which lines their own goods were to follow.

Soup tureen c. 1810–20.

Pair of salts.

Roberts himself tells us something of the early history of the business in a letter written to a Sheffield newspaper in 1843. By about 1765 it is clear that the trade had become considerable: 'There were about six houses engaged in it, and almost all kinds of goods had then become plated metal which had been made of silver.'

Sheffield plate had arrived on the tables of the middle classes, and gave them something which had hitherto been the prerogative of the rich. As the trade was completely new to Sheffield, Roberts tells us, 'workmen at all qualified had to be sought for from London, York, Newcastle, Birmingham and other places. Those who chose to come were, of course, generally indifferent characters, many of them very bad ones; therefore, during the first forty years the journeymen platers were as a body the most unsteady, depraved and idle of all other workmen. The masters could neither do without them or obtain better. They were, therefore, forced to give them high wages, and to wink at all their irregularities.'

This was the state of the industry when Roberts himself, in 1784, together with George Cadman, began his outstandingly successful business career. As the industry grew, better conditions developed. As Roberts points out, a general conviction prevailed from the first among the manufacturers of plated goods at Sheffield that it was in their interest to maintain the quality of their goods: there were exceptions, of course, but they were of no importance.

A firm stand was made against the 'depravity' of the workmen and as time went on circumstances combined to raise their status until in fact it became higher than that of any other kind of workman in Sheffield.

This was true so far as Sheffield was concerned; at Birmingham however, articles 'of a very inferior quality' were manufactured for the foreign market; and this 'has been a means of purifying our plated class at Sheffield'. It had also been a means 'to induce our bad workmen and depraved characters to leave us and go to seek employment there'.

An outstanding exception, of course, was the famous Soho factory created by the Matthew Boultons, father and son, which had grown into one of the wonders of the new industrial age—it was in fact a national showpiece. Matthew Boulton senior had originally set up in Birmingham on Snow Hill as a 'toymaker'—a term covering at that time the manufacture of buttons, boxes and articles of that kind. His son, Matthew, was born in 1728, and entered his father's 'manufactory' at the age of fourteen. On his father's death in 1759 he took over the whole business, and at the age of thirty-two became one of the country's leading manufacturers.

In a city whose name had become synonymous with cheap and sometimes very shoddy wares, he set out to achieve the highest standards of workmanship himself.

He was also anxious to bring under one roof craftsmen from many branches of industry. In this way he would not only be able to reduce overheads but have under his control all the processes of manufacture which went into the goods he sold. He was in fact, like his friend and contemporary, Josiah Wedgwood, one of the pioneers of large scale industrialization. He was later to team up with James Watt in the building of steam engines.

The most important of Boulton's new products was Sheffield and silver plate. He soon became the largest single manufacturer of fused plate in the country, and, almost alone among the Birmingham manufacturers, offered a challenge to the high quality of the Sheffield product. Fused plate was made in Nottingham and London, also in France, Russia and perhaps Germany. The French product, which cannot be dated earlier than about 1770, mostly bears the names of Balaine, Durand, Gandais, and Levrat; marks of some kind are always found. Russian pieces include a samovar, apparently made in what was then known as St Petersburg.

In the year 1784, a new duty on silver put up the price of finished goods made in that metal by 25 per cent. This meant that a silver teapot might now cost £9 instead of £7, a tray £25 rather than £20. These were large sums in those days and the silversmiths tried to meet the situation by lessening the gauge of their metal.

Needless to say, the new impost was of great help to the platers, for the very purpose of their craft was to save on the more precious of the metals they used; and they too lightened the weight of silver used. When further economies had also been made—for example, stamping parts which had previously been raised by hand—they were now in a position to undersell the silversmiths. The French Revolution in 1789 and the years of war which followed brought a check to exports, but trade was opening up steadily in other parts, notably in the New World.

Coats of arms and crests on so many of the surviving pieces show that the gentry and even the nobility were by now accepting services of Sheffield plate as fine properties in their own right, and not as mere imitations of silver. In the upsurge of interest in trade and manufacture they probably took great pride in the fact that English technical ingenuity was so far in front of its rivals. Such foreign plate as was made, chiefly in France, hardly compared in quality with the English work.

2. How it was Made

Sheffield plate had not only to be cheap, but had to look exactly like silver, otherwise it would scarcely be more acceptable than pewter. This called for great ingenuity and very high standards of workmanship. Whatever the style of a piece, whether simple or elaborate, the work itself had to be good, otherwise the public would have none of it. The history of the industry rests, therefore, on improvements of working methods and the introduction of new techniques whereby fused plate could not only rival the work of the silversmiths but perhaps even surpass it.

Plateau with mirror bottom and centre piece, 24 in. long by 20 in. high. Late 18th century.

(a)

(b)

Apart from improved rolling techniques arising out of, first, horse power (by Tudor and Leader), then water power (by Joseph Hancock) and later steam power, the process of fusing remained fairly constant. Even so, the old hand-rolls—they looked rather like household mangles—were kept by for dealing with small pieces.

There were, of course, variations in the proportion of silver to copper. In the early days a very liberal amount of silver was used—say 10 to 12 oz to 8 lb of copper (about 1 to 10)—this was for plating on one side only. There is one early example of very deep-cut engraving used where the silver is as thick as 24 oz to the 8 lb (1 to 5). About 1798 Samuel Roberts tried a very heavy thickness of silver—he called it 'Bell Metal' after his mark—hoping thereby to attract a luxury market and a higher price, but the experiment was not successful, and he reverted to the normal proportion of about 8 to 10 oz to the 8 lb (about 1 to 14) of copper. Later, when 'rubbed-in' shields were introduced, the amount of silver was thinned out to 5 or 7 oz; but items like dish-covers, on account of the extra raising and hammering needed, called for a thickness of, say, 8 oz, for single-sided pieces and 12 oz for double. In the very latest period, when the manufacturers were advertising their 'Sheffield Light Silver Plating', there was a skin of only forty or fifty penny-weights (1 to 60)—rather less than that of electro-plating.

(a) Salt with blue glass liner.
(b) Mustard and (c) salt, 18th century.
(d) Salt, late 18th century.
(e) Egg boiler with sandglass, c. 1795.

HAMMERING AND RAISING

The next important stage in operations was the hammering and raising of a piece into the required shape. This looked the simplest of operations: the workman took a flat sheet of fused metal, and hammered out the shape with strokes of a mallet on a stake. This called for the highest skill, and was the best-paid job in the works. The hammer was so shaped that it left an impression only the size of a pea, and as the workman shaped the piece he had to leave an even surface, capable of being burnished up, so that each stroke had to remove the mark of its predecessor.

Great care had to be taken not to break through the silver coating, especially when it was thin. As in silversmiths' work, this hammering was not solely for the purpose of shaping: it was just as necessary for 'closing' the internal structure of the metal and so toughening it. As with pastry-cooks, hammerers with a 'dry' hand were the best; and like glassblowers, hammerers were born rather than made.

Two cake baskets.
18th century.

SOLDERING

Soldering was also a vital stage in the proceedings. A sheet
would be turned into a cylindrical shape, then soldered with
a 'cramped seam', i.e. a dovetail. After hammering the join
until it was practically invisible, the piece would then be
annealed, or heated, to soften it; then, with a mallet, the
broad outlines—say the neck of a jug—would be 'shaped
in', after which the steel hammer would again come into use
for bringing out the full subtlety of the form required.

There were two methods of soldering, soft and hard. Soft
solder called for lead and tin; consequently not so great a
heat was required. With hard solder, using silver and brass,
very much greater lasting properties were given. It was
employed a great deal in the early days before thin silver
mounts and threaded edges came in, and ran the risk of
being melted in the heat. Samuel Roberts, speaking of his
father's partner, John Winter, who specialized in candlesticks, says that 'he would not suffer any soft solder to be
used, but only silver solder'. As a result, it seems, Winter's
workmen, in their pride, used to call workmen in other
factories 'soft-gob smiths'. Before 1784 some of these candlestick makers put their parts together entirely with soft
solder.

DOUBLE PLATING

In the very early days, as we have seen, pieces were generally silvered on one side only. There were good reasons for this: silver was expensive; there were many articles where a silver surface on both sides was not really essential—such as the undersides of salvers and trays or the insides of dish warmers. These could just as easily and effectively be coated with tin. With hollow ware the method employed was to clean the piece thoroughly, then coat the outside with glue and whitening so that the tin would not damage the outer silvered surface. After the piece had been heated the tin was poured inside the article until it entirely covered the copper surface. With flat pieces like salvers the tin was floated on to the surface, then wiped off carefully with a piece of soft linen.

The earliest form of double plating seems to have been the two-sided salvers and inkstands where the borders or swages are made from two pieces of fused plated metal laid back to back, thus giving plated surfaces on both sides. Joseph Hancock is said to have made his tankards in this way. But this technique was used long after the introduction of double plating—some articles so made even have a

Cake basket, 1760–1770.

tinned underside plate—and it is evident that the technique was used to give an article greater strength and not merely for the purpose of showing a silver surface on both sides.

Frederick Bradbury takes the view that double plating came into use somewhere between 1763 and 1770. Such articles as dishes, cups, beakers and other articles constantly in use for eating and drinking—always bearing in mind that inevitable comparison with silver—would benefit by being plated on both sides. If this cost more to do, then the customer would surely be induced to pay more for a better article.

Double plating was especially useful with the mounts used on salvers. It would have been difficult to strike out decorative mounts of such thickness that they would stand up to hard wear on their own, whereas by placing together the two pieces, the mounts would not only be stronger but it would be possible to give them much finer detail. The edges would be soldered with tin so as to preserve the colour of the metal. After scraping and burnishing scarcely anything could be seen of the join.

DIE STAMPING

In Sheffield, with its long history of cutlery manufacture, it would have been surprising if the platers had not made great use of dies and die-stamping. They were cut from steel by means of small hardened chisels, like those of a sculptor or intaglio gem cutter. In the early days the dies had been of softer metal, which allowed only a few pieces to be stamped, after which the piece had to be chased up by hand; this, it has been suggested, accounts for the great dissimilarity of patterns in the earliest pieces.

The dies were used in a machine rather like a guillotine, having a heavy stamp between two uprights, originally worked by a wheel and pulley system which the operator controlled by a stirrup on which he could place his weight: in the later days, of course, the operation was carried out by power.

SWAGING

The process of swaging, as used in other metal-working industries, played no less a part in the making of articles like trays, dishes, decanters, stands and various parts of other pieces in Sheffield plate. The swage looked rather like a denture in its mould. The movable part was in fact called a jaw, with the design cut into it in relief, while the bottom, where the same shape would be seen in intaglio, was called the face. The silver surface of the piece was protected by means of a piece of leather, whereupon the top of the jaw was either pushed down with the hand or struck with a hammer. The piece was then sent to the flat hammerers and thence on to the mounters. A very large number of swages were kept in stock, giving every possible variety of pattern.

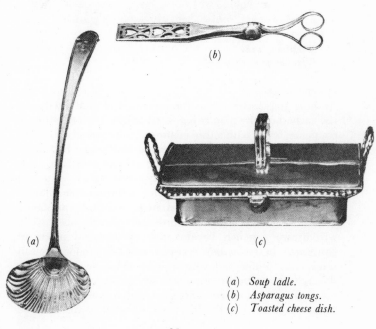

(*b*)

(*a*)

(*c*)

(*a*)   Soup ladle.
(*b*)   Asparagus tongs.
(*c*)   Toasted cheese dish.

(a) *Monteith c. 1780.*
(b) *Wine coaster c. 1810.*

PLATED WIRE

Another step forward was the invention of plated wire. In
the early days the platers had used hollow tubing, either of
copper or brass, with a thin coating of fused metal around it.
But this wore very badly, and some better way had to be
found. Around the year 1768 the rolling mills began to
supply solid plated wire in strips; a process was patented
about that time by George Whateley, a Birmingham plater.

It was not easy to make at first, in fact, it presented
greater problems than the ordinary plated sheets. The
wire-drawer's bench became one of the vital pieces of
equipment in the factory. A copper bar, say 5 in long by 1 in
thick, was pulled out into a long string by drawing it
through the 'whortle'—a plate on the draw-bench with
holes of various shapes and sizes which would gradually
bring the wire into the form and diameter wanted. One

then bent over this a thin strip of silver 1/32 in in thickness, fused the two metals together, then, using the 'whortle' again, drew them out into a long thin string—much as with millefiore glass.

This made an enormous improvement in the workmanship on dishes, tureens, cake-baskets and other items with what was called a 'self mount', i.e., where the swages and mounts were cut as one, and therefore needed strengthening. But the outstanding virtue of the new wire was that attractive patterns could be made up in it.

(a) *Tankard c. 1780, after a silver design of about 1725.*
(b) *Wine coaster c. 1780.*
(c) *Soup ladle.*

(a)

(b)

(c)

An important development of this technique gave the platers the silver-threaded edge, which gave longer life to an article by protecting its edges. As already mentioned, Samuel Roberts and George Cadman were the first to make use of this device.

In this case the wire was of solid silver. It was, as usual, drawn through a 'whortle', but the thin strip of silver was not only made exactly the size of the edge to be covered, but in the same operation it became grooved, thus facilitating the soldering on. In this way an edge could never wear away and reveal the copper beneath.

It provided a valuable selling point, and platers who used it would sometimes draw attention to this fact by stamping on such pieces, alongside their name and mark the word: 'SILVER EDGES'. Matthew Boulton also took up the process, with highly successful results: he would sometimes put the words 'SILVER BORDERS' alongside his mark.

SILVER MOUNTS

After silver-threaded edges, silver mounts were a logical enough step. It was about the year 1789 that they came into more general use, superseding the old mounts in plated metal. On dishes, waiters, tureens, salts, etc, mounts were struck up from long thin strips of silver filled with a solder of lead and tin. At first quite simple borders were used—the plain, the thread, the bead, the slant gadroon—but later the process was used for more elaborate scalloping and shell work.

There were several ways of putting on these mounts. By one method the edge of the piece where the mount was to be placed would be filed thin and then turned back, so concealing the copper edge. In another, called by collectors the 'turn-over edge' or the 'lapped-over edge', the edge of the piece was not filed, but covered with a U-shaped thread of silver and attached with soft solder; the copper edge having been covered, the mount could then be added. When this method has been used a thin band of silver can be seen on the underside of the piece. This edge tends to come off; and perhaps for this reason it was once called by the makers the 'sign of poverty' edge. Early pieces would also sometimes be mounted by leaving an edge or 'fash' on the mount itself. After being placed in position, this edge would be turned underneath. The cheapest type of plate shows a bevelled edge which, instead of a silver edge, reveals the solder.

Samuel Roberts, having played such an important part in introducing silver edges, took out a patent in 1824 which was designed to make them unnecessary. His specification explains the disadvantages of the then existing methods: by one, the raw edge of the copper was frequently exposed to view; by the second, the silver thread gave away the fact that the article had been plated. His method was:

> after filing the edge of the article to nearly the shape (but somewhat less) of the ornamented indented silver edging, to hard solder a silver thread of the required strength upon the said edge, and then to flat it with a hammer upon a metal stake to the breadth and strength required, and so the outer edge will extend a little beyond the ornamented silver edge, which is then to be soft soldered on in the usual way. The projecting part of the hard soldered silver edge, which extends beyond the ornamented silver edge, is then to be filed off, and the two edges burnished together till the joining disappears. By this method it is obvious that a workman will scarcely be able at first sight to distinguish a plated from a silver article, and that the edges themselves will endure almost as long as solid silver ones, without the copper becoming at all perceptible.

Roberts's claim was fully justified, and in much of the later plating the edges offer hardly any means of identifying ware which had been plated.

REPOUSSE WORK

The repoussé work or embossing carried out in the early days was called by the trade 'chasing in high relief' to distinguish it from the flat chasing which was in use all

(a) *Inkstand and candle-stand combined. Original silver design by William Darkeratt* (?) *1724–25.*
(b) *Inkstand c. 1780.* (c) *Taper stand.*

through the era of fused plate. In the former process, of course, the article is 'worked up' from the back as well as the front. Much hollow ware was decorated in this way—notably coffee pots, two-handled cups, hot-water jugs, tea-caddies and other articles—using a snarling iron. This was a bar with one end twisted down, secured in a vice: the other pointed up into the piece, and when the iron was struck at the end near the vice, the hammer point at the top would bounce up inside the piece and raise the shapes required. Afterwards the article could be chased from the other side by filling it with pitch and indenting inwards with a chasing tool. The embossed work usually consisted of flowers and leaf shapes.

Fluting was a form of embossing, use being made first of the snarling iron to raise the design from below: a piece of hollow ware could be filled with pitch and the fluting brought out from the other side. Flutes could be spiral or straight and of different lengths; while flat and full flutes might be combined. Flat fluting was a feature of the early work.

FLAT CHASING

This was almost a speciality of Sheffield plate, although it was used in early silverwork. But whereas the silversmiths could afford to cut out their chased designs with an engraving tool, actually removing small particles of silver from the surface, the plater, with his thin skin of silver, could only indent it. He would place a piece of flatware—say a salver—in a bed of warm pitch, then trace out his design with chalk and a steel pointer. He then selected a variety of small punches and 'matted' over some areas, such as the veins of leaves or the petals of flowers. In the case of hollow ware, the article could either be worked against a stake, as in flat-hammering, or filled up inside with pitch and worked on a sand cushion.

Candelabrum, 18th century, with late additions.

BRIGHT-CUT ENGRAVING

The kind of engraving called 'bright cut', much used by silversmiths, came into fashion on plated wares for teapots, coffee pots, teapot stands, waiters and the like about the year 1789. This technique, which is rather like chip-carving, calls for slanting cuts at different angles; and after the sharp edges have been worn down by time it is difficult to distinguish from flat chasing—although with the latter it should be possible to find the reverse marks under the piece. But shallow though the cuts were in bright-cut engraving, it was possible only when a specially heavy coat of silver had been used.

PIERCED WORK

One of the most attractive forms of decoration in silver, of course, is pierced work, where intricate and elaborate patterns are let into the metal. The platers could not imitate the process used by the silversmiths, i.e. fretsaw work, for this would have exposed the copper edge in the 'sandwich'. They therefore evolved—somewhere about 1765, it is thought—a variation on the stamp hammer, whereby a small hardened tool, shaped according to the effect required, was fixed in a punching machine, and an appropriate bed laid below the work. This 'fly piercing' had the effect of squeezing the metal between punch and bed, and so

28

Candlesticks:
(a) c. 1760, (b)
c. 1780, (c) and
(d) 1790–1800,
(e) c. 1820–30,
with telescopic
stem.

tended to pull the silver over the copper rather than leave it exposed. Some of the fine patterns made possible by this process, used in conjunction with other technical devices described, may be seen in these pages.

SHIELDS

Teapots, coffee pots and urns often had silver bands soldered on to take engraving, and an adaptation of this process brought about a most ingenious solution to the problem of engraving crests and coats-of-arms on Sheffield plate.

Buyers of plate who bore arms inevitably required an engraved crest as in silver; and if Sheffield plate was to hold its own in this distinguished company it had to make similar provision for family pride. The manufacturers could themselves have worked in the shields or crests by flat chasing; but in most cases they sold their wares through retailers in distant parts, and although there were silver engravers everywhere, the effect of their vigorous scalloping out would have been fatal to plated ware. To send the wares back to the factory to be flat chased was far too troublesome and risky, so before the piece left the factory some kind of provision had to be made for the engraver in distant parts to work the design.

At first the only answer was to provide a thicker skin of

silver—say 12 oz to 8 lb. Then it occurred to someone that if a small shield of extra heavily plated metal were let in at the place where a crest was to be engraved, this would make it possible for the rest of the silver skin to be in a much lighter weight.

By the earliest process a piece of the metal was cut out of the front of the article, and an extra-strong plated piece hard-soldered into its place. After scraping away the surplus metal, then hammering and burnishing, the join was hardly visible, especially when a wavy line was lightly engraved around it to engage the eye.

Ingenious as it may have been, soldering-in was a fairly costly operation, and the makers usually made an extra charge when a shield had to be provided. But the next step—the 'rubbed-in' shield—solved the cost problem. The same 'Wilks' who was responsible for the first method of plating wire is credited with the invention. This time fine silver of about 4-gauge thickness was used, with tapered edges, and after being heated lightly in the flame it was applied over the place where the shield was required; then the whole was heated up on an open fire until it was red hot. The workman now began to burnish backwards and forwards over the face of the shield and around its edges until the fine silver fused into the standard silver on the surface of the piece. After further hammering and burnishing, no sign could be seen of anything having been added, still less that a piece of metal had been 'forced' into a flat surface. The difference in the metal is discernible, of course, when a piece has become tarnished or when breathed on because of the quite different properties of 'fine', i.e. nearly pure, and sterling standard silver, which is ·925 parts of fine alloyed silver.

The job, as will be realized, was an extremely difficult one and it was a supreme test of a man's capacity with the tools of the plater to be able to rub in a shield successfully.

FRENCH PLATING
The original process of plating was, as we have seen, one

where the silver coating was given to the article after it had been made up. This was called by the platers French plating, because of its origin in France. The same term was used for a process of 'patching up' used by the fused platers. Where blemishes occurred in the surface of a costly piece, say a blister, which exposed the copper below, and no hard wear was likely to occur in the place, the workmen would take thin foils of pure silver from a sheaf; and after heating them and cleaning the place to be repaired they would burnish them down one after another under pressure. The repair was almost invisible except when tarnished, for, as with the rubbed-in shields, the metal was pure silver rather than alloyed, and the difference showed.

SPINNING

This was a process which came late into the industry. It was an alternative to stamping a large shape out with a die. The shape required was expressed in a kind of wooden template called a chuck, which was mounted on a lathe. The workman, taking a sheet of fused metal, fixed it to the chuck with a loose pin then, with his burnish, gradually forced the metal on to the revolving chuck so that it took its shape. Constant annealing was necessary, but in fact a piece could be spun up in a very short space of time. This could be a great advantage when a new pattern was wanted quickly, since die cutting could take up valuable time.

In the 1820s a great many spun pieces came into Britain from France, where the art had been developed much earlier. Frederick Bradbury says that, in fact, the French were always better spinners than the English because of their method of working. In England, it seems, the workmen stood up to their work, and therefore used only their shoulders and arms; whereas the Frenchmen sat on revolving stools and—so to speak—swung their whole weight on to the points of their burnishes. This same process, of course, was highly developed in subsequent days of electro-plating.

3. The Wares

Most spectacular of the wares in Sheffield plate are those designed for the table; and perhaps the most splendid of these are the large épergnes and centre-pieces where every resource of the trade was called on. In typical lists of productions these combinations of centre and side dishes, accompanied by such auxiliaries as muffineers, mustards, salts and cruet-stands, were given first place. They were certainly not cheap: a typical specimen cost from fifteen to twenty-five guineas wholesale. Alongside them stood the épergne of wirework on a revolving stand, with perhaps eight baskets for carrying fruit, sweetmeats and flowers. Cut glass was liberally used.

Many of those which survive today are in surprisingly good condition: as they were used on special occasions only, perhaps they have escaped the frequent cleaning given to pieces in more constant use. The old glass has often gone, of course, but nowadays this can be remedied. Certainly these pieces *need* cut glass—after all, they were born in the great age of the English and Irish crystal cutting.

TABLE WARE

Of the larger dinner table wares, vegetable dishes are usually round, and because of the vast distance which often lay between kitchen and dining-room, they might have an outer jacket to contain hot water and keep the food warm; the handle was unscrewed and the boiling water poured down a hollow connecting with the jacket. In other models there might be a screw plug, with the dish itself divided by three removable partitions.

Candle sconces, snuffers and trays and taper stand. 18th and 19th centuries.

ARGYLES AND HOT-PLATES

The same concern for keeping food hot is shown in what was called the Argyle, designed for holding gravy. It had its name, it is said, from a Duke of Argyll who devised this method whereby he could have his gravy hot.

Some resemble teapots, having a separate internal chamber for the hot water round which the gravy warmed itself. Another form is like a hot-water jug with a double lining or jacket: the water was poured down the lip and the gravy flowed into an inside compartment. The spout went right through the water jacket, so that the gravy did not get cooled off as it poured out.

Sauce tureens are sometimes fitted with a double jacket in this way, especially the Adam types in which the characteristic high looped handles are hollow, and there are two small catches at the top of the handles concealing small openings down which hot water can be poured.

Other methods of retaining heat are shown in the great variety of entrée dishes, which seem to have come on the· scene rather late, say after about 1785. They were usually accompanied by a warmer of some kind; the earlier types have a hot iron on a metal framework in the base; later the dish might be fitted inside a hot-water container. Many of these dishes must have spent much of their time in inns and hotels: in the catalogues they are called double dishes, steak dishes and hash dishes.

The earliest of the tureens are on the small side: they are

Salver with chased work, 1820–30, 24 in across.

sometimes called 'oval canoes' but although they seem to have been made in large numbers they are not easy to find today.

DISH-COVERS

Large covers for dishes containing joints or fowl came into use, it seems, around the year 1800. A few years later they were available in sets, the sizes ranging from 10 in up to 24 in. The early plain ones were presumably used chiefly on the sideboards of coaching inns, but the attention given to design in the later ones and the presence of rubbed-in armorial shields suggests that they soon found their way into private houses.

They are not infrequently to be found, looking rather lost, in general antique shops, where their identity as Old Sheffield Plate is not always recognized. I myself found one for thirty shillings, which, after breathing on it in the right place, I found to have a shield, although it was not engraved. Nowadays, they are sometimes fitted with wires as hanging flower-baskets, or cut in half to make wall flower pockets. There are smaller covers intended for china dishes or plates.

BREAKFAST AND SUPPER

The breakfast dish is still in use in many houses, complete with its cover and warmer. Supper services are more rarely found, for they could be really immense affairs—perhaps the most expensive of any of the wares. A complete supper service—intended to keep food and drink warm and ready for a party after a visit to the opera or the theatre, or home-coming from a ball or reception—was one of the grandest assemblies of fused plate. But very few of these large affairs can have survived.

Much the same applies to the grandiose 'Tea Equipage Compleat' or 'Tea and Coffee Machine' as shown on page 51 : one doubts if there are any other specimens of this still extant. The topmost of the urns was for water, kept hot by the spirit lamp underneath, and the two lower ones held tea and coffee respectively. These also each had their spirit lamp—which sounds reasonable enough for the coffee but one wonders what the tea tasted like after stewing so long. This piece, by Daniel Holy, Wilkinson and Co., was of extra thick plating and sold originally at £30.

Alongside the covered dishes would perhaps have been some of the many types of toast-racks, made up from plated wire, as well as egg frames, egg boilers and another piece of gadgetry we do not seem to find a place for today, the old cheese toaster. In using this you cut your cheese and bread into thin slices and put them in these divided dishes, which were then put before the fire; the lid could be kept up by a chain contrivance, which helped to reflect the heat of the fire on to the toasting cheese and bread. Most of them had hot water compartments as well. There are combined

Tray with repoussé work, 18th century.

épergnes and cruets, egg frames with spoons, salt and pepper and toast-racks with egg cups.

COFFEE-POTS AND JUGS

Coffee-pots came pear-shaped at first, like the contemporary silver wares. There are a good many of them about, and they are usually in good condition, being extra heavily plated. There is also the coffee-jug, distinguished by its lip, which can be either square and bulbous or with straight tapering sides: these are sometimes called 'biggins'. There is also a smaller side-handled coffee-pot with either a lip or a spout, holding from three-quarters of a pint to a pint and a half, with a stand and a small lamp underneath.

Chocolate-pots were not made in great numbers by the platers; perhaps this drink was for the most part preferred by the users of silver. They appear in a manufacturer's list of 1774, but very few are mentioned in later years. They, too, had the elongated pear shape in the first days, and after that moved up on to a higher stand.

CRUETS AND CONDIMENTS

Cruets in plate survive in great variety. The simplest of them hold combinations of mustard, salt and pepper pots; then there is an elaboration into vinegar and sauces. There are hundreds of varieties of bottle patterns, for of course in this department the glassmakers really let themselves go and produced all the successive styles in miniature.

Condiments on their own have always attracted collectors, partly because they are small pieces and therefore more readily gathered, but also for the reason just mentioned; that they offer in small compass an illustration of styles and techniques in plating. Salts have always attracted good prices, and even more so mustards. Those with pierced work are the most popular, and justifiably so, for they are the most attractive items, and when in good condition their excellent workmanship makes them very difficult to distinguish from silver.

Not at all unlike the cruet frames, though usually much

larger, are the liquor frames for sets of bottles or decanters. Bradbury says that in his time there was not much use for them and that they could then be bought at a tenth the price of cruet frames. Claret jugs are among the most handsome of pieces, but they are not very easy to come by.

TANKARDS AND MUGS

Many of the platers specialized in making tankards, both for private use and for inns and taverns: some made nothing else. Thomas Law, Nathaniel Smith, John Love and Josephus Smith were all prolific makers. Platers were also quick to cash in on a regulation changing the legal measure to the Winchester standard, offering to 'enlarge old silver and plated quarts, pints and half pints, in the neatest, completest, most expeditious and cheapest manner'.

This Winchester measure is a reminder that in Saxon times the seat of government in England was at Winchester; and the Winchester bushel was used in England until 1824, when the imperial bushel was made legal measure. The old wine gallon under the Winchester system, which was about five-sixths of the Imperial gallon, is still the standard measure in the United States.

Some tankards from inns and taverns are stamped 'IM' for Imperial Measure, others with the Royal Crown and initials, and in the case of tankards attested in Sheffield, the town's double cross-arrows mark. These have the domed and double-domed lids familiar in pewter, and while the early ones take the contemporary cylindrical form with out-spreading foot, the later styles follow the bulbous forms of the late eighteenth century. Some of those made in the first days have the dummy silver marks referred to elsewhere. There is some dispute about the purpose of the slits which are sometimes to be found under the handles of tankards: some say they were a precaution taken in the soldering; others that they were there so that one could whistle down them for more beer. There are a great many pint mugs, some with two handles.

Another collectable line in its own right is the wine coaster. They are also called bottle stands, decanter stands or bottle trays. They were designed to protect the table when a bottle of wine was being passed along, and because of this usually had a wooden base. Few were made in the very earliest period, but towards the end of the eighteenth century they were extremely popular, and the platers put every effort into making them look attractive and impressive. Today, with the great increase in wine drinking, they are much in demand.

This, it should be remembered, was the great period of Anglo-Irish cut-glass, and nothing could better be contrived to show off a fine decanter than a silvery holder which slid from one end of the table to another in the soft light of candles. There are literally hundreds of patterns, many of them making the most felicitous use of pierced work.

As an extension of the coaster there is the wine wagon: and according to Bradbury we owe its invention to the already-mentioned Sir Edward Thomason. In his memoirs he notes that Lord Rolle being sent to him by George IV, to see if he could solve the problem whereby 'his noble guests who sat on either side of him were constrained to rise from their seats to pass the wine', he suggested to Lord Rolle that decanter stands on wheels were the only method to be adopted:

and as I hold the beautiful dies containing the victories of the late war, forty in number, from the landing in Portugal to the capture of Paris and the settling of Napoleon at St. Helena, I recommend to place these medals around the flat but perpendicular edges of the bottle stands which would fill up four and thereby adapting them to two wagons, the whole made of silver and richly gilt and each wagon to have beautifully ornamented wheels. His Majesty expressed his entire approbation and some time afterwards he presented them to the Duke of Wellington.

But, Bradbury adds, notwithstanding this story, wine wagons not very dissimilar are to be met with in both silver and Sheffield plate which were apparently made late in the eighteenth century.

THE WARWICK VASE

Possibly the most distinguished article concerned with drinking, however, was the wine cooler or 'ice pail' in which the bottle of Rhenish or Champagne awaited the pleasure of the company. Some of these are beautifully designed, showing all the forms of the late eighteenth century in

(*a*) *Chocolate pot.* (*b*) *Coffee pot c. 1760.*

(*c*) *Coffee pot c. 1765.* (*d*) *Hot water jug, late 18th century, with simulated silver hallmarks.*

Three sugar basins, with blue glass liners, 18th century.

considerable state. The most famous of them was the Warwick Vase, a highly ornate affair after an original in white
marble in the grounds of Warwick Castle.

Trays, already mentioned under making and method,
called for first-rate workmanship because of the heavy wear
expected of them. They were among the earliest of the
pieces made by Joseph Hancock and there is one in
existence which was given by Thomas Boulsover to his
daughter Mary. Throughout the history of fused plating
they were made in every sort of form, perhaps with even
more variety than in silver.

POTATO RINGS

Among the odder kinds of articles to be found in Sheffield
plate are the famous so-called 'potato rings'. Nobody seems
to know quite why they are so called, unless it is that they
were particularly popular in silver among Irish buyers; but
if you think of them simply as dish rings, made to support a
dish on the table, the mystery disappears. It has also been
suggested that they were used as stands for china and
porcelain punch bowls, to protect the polished surface of
side tables. They are treated in various ways: they can be
chased in high or low relief, have pierced work or merely be

made up of rings which support a wire holder. Since the Sheffield platers' general catalogues do not show these articles, it is thought that they were dealt with in a separate one for the Irish market.

TEA-TABLE WARES

The Georgian tea-table offered many opportunities to the maker of fused plate. The most ubiquitous item, of course, was the teapot, but it does not seem to have been made in large numbers by the platers until after about 1770. Something is said about their styles in Chapter 4. At first designed with stands, they later acquired ball feet. Apparently the claw and ball foot was not popular with the platers—perhaps it presented manufacturing difficulties.

Teapots made as part of a service are said to have usually been given all-metal handles; but those sold singly tended to be in some material designed to insulate the heat—stained wood, ebony, compressed horn. There are ivory knobs, some very attractively stained in green and carved as pineapples.

Tea urns seem to have been in production from the 1760s and were brought out when the hostess gathered her friends round her in her retiring room after dinner. Many of them were of only two or three quarts capacity—which are the ones now most sought after: later they grew to great sizes with every conceivable elaboration. They could be heated either by means of a hot 'box iron' placed in a compartment inside the vessel or by a spirit lamp. The hostess would have her teapot beside her, together with caddies closely following the same style, if not actually made *en suite*. They might be divided into two for black and green tea, and, this being a costly luxury, they would either have a lock or be contained in a lockable tea-chest. Tea kettles are rarely found: perhaps the habit of using them pre-dated the plating days.

Cream jugs were also made *en suite* with teapots and caddies, but sugar-bowls and baskets seem to have been

thought of as something apart. About 1775 they appear
with pierced work and other decoration, the contents being
in a glass liner. They are sometimes called sugar pails.
There are others entirely made up in glass wire work except
for a band of pierced decoration, with a cover of the same
wirework. There are also solid sugar boxes, perhaps square,
en suite with oval caddies in a chest.

CUTLERY

Spoons and forks exist in fused plate as has already been
mentioned on page 10. Teaspoons and sugar-tongs were
beaten out of drawn wire, with flat chasing on their shanks,
but they tended to lose their silvering.

CHURCH PLATE

Like the pewterers, the Sheffield platers supplied their
quota of wares for the Church. Altar candlesticks, com-
munion cups, incense burners, ciboriums, altar cruets were
among the articles mentioned in a catalogue issued by the
firm of Gainsford, who used the marks of an elephant's
head. Like those in pewter, all these articles usually have
austere lines.

TOBACCO AND CIGAR BOXES

The smoker was not overlooked by the platers. Tobacco
boxes had been made by the silversmiths almost from the
earliest days of nicotine in England, and for the humbler
smoker there was a vast selection of boxes in lead and brass.
The platers put their skill to good use in giving their boxes
the totally airtight lid needed to keep the tobacco in good
order.

The pipe lighter was another popular product of the
platers. One pattern had a separate copper lining for
holding some glowing combustible material like peat: it
might be screwed to a plate, so that it could be left on the
table without causing damage. The tinder box was another
smoker's requisite; some have a nozzle for a taper stick on
their tops.

Sheffield plate lived out its life in the age of candlelight. Throughout the whole period, most people, from the humblest to the most exalted, relied for their lighting on some form of wax or tallow candle. At one end of the scale there was the simple chamber candlestick, with its snuffer scissors and douter cap, at hand on the hall table to light you to bed; at the other was the great candelabra on the Adam sideboard or the long dining-table, throwing its soft light over brilliant glass and white linen.

In the earliest of the candlesticks the parts can sometimes look misshapen. They were made of thick metal, perhaps struck up from rough dies, and the collets hoop-soldered together and swaged into shape afterwards. About the year 1765, however, they began to be made entirely from cast dies, without swaging.

Tea caddies, late 18th century.

An outstanding feature of the whole fused plate candlestick family is the number of ingenious devices worked out to give users some kind of service or convenience. Bradbury lists no fewer than 34 patents on candlesticks and snuffers between 1749 and 1842, when fused plating ended. As he points out, one could make an interesting collection of snuffers showing the different kinds of dodges that were offered by the manufacturers so that the unwanted piece of charred wick—which was not then self-consuming—could be neatly snipped off and caught in its little box.

Most of these snuffers, somewhat exceptionally, have some sort of indication, by mark or name, of their origin; a great many of them were actually close-plated, this having been found by many of the makers to be a more practical method.

Those interested in displaying a variety of styles in a single type of piece will find what they seek in the snuffer tray. They are eagerly collected; and one of the sad things is how often small dealers, on coming across these pieces and finding the copper showing through, rush them straight off to the electro-platers for re-plating; after which, of course, they lose for ever their old mellow tint and acquire the cold hard colour of modern plating. But they take a good deal of spoiling; and perhaps they are the most practically useful of all the plated wares—as trays for sweetmeats, trinkets and other items.

Candlesticks could be telescopic in a number of ways, making it possible to raise and lower them at the convenience of the user. The normal method was to fit a cloth lining in the slides, so that the pillars were not scratched by friction between the moving parts. Eckhardt's patent, which varied from the others in having adjustable brass collets fitted as a slide, was very early in the field, perhaps leading all the others. Another variation was based on the principle of the Archimedean screw: the candle was fixed on a small spike in the base of the candlestick; to raise it you simply screwed up the pillar, which lifted the capital. Firms tended

44

to specialize in candlestick making—as we have seen already in the case of Winters.

The taper candlestick is a pleasant miniature version of its larger brother. It was used at the tea-table, partly to burn aromatically scented candles to sweeten the air in the room, partly for lighting. It often forms part of the whole set of writing apparatus on the desk, perhaps standing on the lid of the little box containing the wafers used for sealing the

Teapots:
(a) *late 18th century*
(b) *with hollywood knop and ebonised handle (re-silvered) and*
(c) *in revived rococo style, with chased body and claw feet, by Watson & Bradbury, 1818.* (Sheffield City Museum)

45

(a)   *Cream jug, late 18th century.*   (b)   *Toast rack c. 1790.*
(c)   *Sugar basin, late 18th century.*

letters: it would provide heat for melting sealing-wax for the seals so often used in those days for signing letters, and later for sealing them. Another piece of lighting apparatus used about this time was the wax winder, with a handle and bar, whereby the coil of wax, as it was used, could be unwound: a variation on this was the bougie box, which contained the wax coil inside it: you pulled it out by hand.

Candelabra seem to have been on the scene by the 1770s at least. The various branches and parts were not only interchangeable in themselves, but also with épergnes—as these latter were themselves to be found in combination with cruets, etc.

With these candelabra, much subtlety lies in the balance and height of the arms in relation to the columns and to the size and placing of the nozzles. Here the connoisseur with an eye for design can learn to use it.

INKSTANDS

Inkstands, of course, engaged the attention of platers from the earliest days. There is one type which is modelled on the globe, standing on a pedestal; another plays variations on the idea of a cruet. Among the more delightful of them are those with a boat-shaped tray—with bottles or boxes for pounce or sand flanking the ink container.

We have by no means exhausted the list of items made in Sheffield plate: they must, in fact, have been more numerous than those in any other single metal. There are ceremonial maces, presentation trowels for Freemasons, barbers' dishes, flasks, coach lamps, lemon-strainers, knitting sheaths, wine-strainers, mutton-holders, dish wedges, fish-slices, shaving lamps, ear-trumpets, table bells, honey hives, sugar crushers, key escutcheons and handles on tea caddies and knife boxes—the list is endless, and doubtless items are being newly discovered all the time.

MOUNTED WARES

An important class of Sheffield plate combines the fused metal with glass and pottery. The firm of Thomas Law & Co. already mentioned specialized in mounting the fine jasper wares then being produced by Staffordshire potters led by Josiah Wedgwood and John Turner, William Adams and others. Sheffield plate mounts are also to be found on the well-known stoneware hunting jugs, with their relief modelling of horsemen and hounds.

With some of these pieces, the mount consists simply of a rim, though some may have a cover as well. In all cases the fused fittings consort admirably with the fine stonewares produced by these firms. Here is where the plate collector may find his quarry lurking in some unsuspected 'earth' like a general china shop.

Glass collectors will also have come across their own treasured material accompanied by Sheffield plate. Like the silversmiths, the platers made great use of the plain crystal or tinted glass liners used in condiments, sugar baskets and other items, notably in the famous 'Bristol blue'—not all of which came from Bristol, it may be mentioned. Needless to say, pieces of plate which still have their original glass accessories are most highly valued and sought after by connoisseurs.

4. The Styles

When first looking at Old Sheffield Plate, the connoisseur of styles may find himself a little lost, for it is extremely difficult, and sometimes very misleading, to try to date Sheffield plate by its style alone. This is aggravated by rather confusing terms which are sometimes used by collectors and dealers: their divisions generally start with something they call 'Queen Anne'; and this is followed by 'Early Georgian', 'Empire' and then just 'Late'.

In several types, notably, for example, teapots, the styles can often go in reverse to the normal sequence—or at first glance may appear to do so. The reason is not far to seek. Firstly, plating was an imitative art: the models already existed in silver and pottery. On the other hand, it was, as we have seen, also a craft which was developing all the time; and what was technically impossible in one generation often proved perfectly feasible in the next. There could thus have been a strong temptation to go back on one's tracks and imitate something from the past.

Combination interchangeable coffee and teapot. (Sheffield City Museum)

Another factor may well have been a decided difference between the tastes of those who bought silver and those who took the substitute. So far as style was concerned, silver and porcelain kept pretty much abreast of each other (note, for example, the famous 'Goat and Bee' jugs and other early Chelsea wares based on silver patterns).* But Old Sheffield Plate, in its early days at all events, was likely to have been bought by those who were not too closely in touch with the latest mode; and just as the Worcester china factory, with its keen eye on the rising provincial taste, always kept a generation or two behind Dresden or Sèvres, so the platers could be equally skilled in divining the current requirements of their market.

There may, too, have been practical reasons: as that the family silver had been sold, or some had, and replacements were wanted in the same style.

What has become known as the 'Queen Anne' style in plate is not to be equated with the same term in silver or furniture; that is with simple, even austere, forms tastefully and restrainedly ornamented, but having great sophistication of outline. Typical are the straight-sided tankards and pear-shaped teapots in silver. What is meant by this term in Sheffield plate, it appears, is a kind of 'primitive', sometimes of a certain clumsiness, but none the less full of character and charm. The pieces are usually plain, or have some shallow fluting and spirals of threading: they seem to give the feeling of being the individual production of one man rather than of a group making different parts or carrying out different functions.

Another type generally classed along with the foregoing is more sophisticated in its general appearance, but it goes in for oblong or oval shapes, has much more strongly emphasized fluting and gadrooning, and in fact seems to be in the same mood as a great deal of George I silver.

'Early Georgian', on the other hand, moves away from this position and becomes much more what one would prefer to call 'Mid-Georgian', 'Chippendale' or even

49

* SEE *Chelsea and Derby China* in this series.

'Rococo'. It takes on the heavier elaboration in silver of Paul Lamerie and his followers, with much embossing and chasing, especially of flowers, spiral fluting and strong 'Chippendale' scrolls. Another type discards this fluting but has flowers in a different style; they may be set out in swags. There is also a great deal of piercing, sometimes geometrical, but still very much following the Lamerie styles of a generation before.

By 'Late Georgian' is presumably meant the 'Adam' style, with its rediscovery of classicism. The words 'Adams' and 'Adam' have been rather confusingly used in writing of Sheffield plate, and it may be helpful if one points out that here we are not discussing the work of the Adams family of potters (although they did in fact make great use of the 'Adam' style) but of the influence of the brothers Robert and John Adam, the first named of whom came back to this country from Rome in the year 1768 with his brilliant and original designer's mind full of the classical styles which were then exciting Europe—and which have often been referred to in this series of books.

One of the most popular forms in the new style was the classical urn. It appeared as covered cups, tea caddies, tea urns, tureens and other wares; and the same shape is to be seen in other fields, especially the Wedgwood jasper ware already mentioned—which is often mounted with plate. Indeed, the platers may well have been influenced by that great potter's early adoption of the style.

Another common feature was the architectural column, in all its various 'orders'. This found immediate and lasting expression in the huge variety of candlesticks made by the platers. As with the silversmiths, their interpretations of the 'orders'—Corinthian, Ionic, Egyptian, etc—frequently strayed away from strict architectural tenets; but the early efforts of the Sheffield men in this department showed a natural good taste. Of John Winter's candlesticks, Samuel Roberts said: 'Perhaps none more chaste have since been made.'

Decoration on the new forms usually relied a great deal on the swag of drapery or laurel leaves or the ram's head, expressed with a simple, often noble, elegance which was not entirely remote from the feeling of some late Stuart and Queen Anne work. But as time went on ornateness began to creep on to the simple forms, with heavily embossed medallions and much deep repoussé work. To impress their customers with the value of their work, the platers began to ring changes on the 'orders', mixing features that ought not to be

Tea and coffee machine, 24 in high by 10 in across, 32 lb weight, by D. Holy, Wilkinson & Co. 1798. (Sheffield City Museum)

mixed, and then trying to cover up these fumblings by using the full gamut of 'Empire'—masks, the acanthus leaf, winged lions, even Egyptian sphinxes.

Platers who had followed the silversmiths thus far now seem to have panicked, finding that their customers were beginning to shy away from this particular kind of elaboration. But instead of returning to the simple elegancies of High Adam, which had actually called for more real taste and skill in conception, they either developed very strongly—and very beautifully too—their own speciality of pierced work or they went right back over the years to something like 'Mid-Georgian'. Fluting was revived (though now as a structural thing, e.g. wrythen columns); there were highly chased flowers and shells either on their own or added as embellishments to the gadrooning. We had arrived at what has been called 'Revived Rococo': in other words something very like Rockingham china.

We are left with the 'Late' period: it has also been called the 'Florid', and this perhaps describes it pretty aptly. Now the platers threw in everything they knew—size, elaboration, mixed motifs—and the effect was overwhelming. But there were some fine things produced in the era, especially when, for example, the intricate floral edges were combined with a virtual absence of ornament elsewhere. The craftsmanship, in the better pieces, was certainly superb: never had there been such refinement of casting, such art-concealing art in soldering, such magnificent finishing. It is no wonder that these pieces have survived in many cases looking as fresh as the day on which they were made.

5. The End of Fused Plate

Before Sheffield plate was finally overtaken by electrolysis, there was a 'transitional' period, say between 1830 and 1840, during which a good many of the platers used 'German silver' or 'nickel silver' as their foundation metal in preference to copper. This alloy of copper, zinc and nickel, introduced into Britain from Germany, although more expensive than copper, was much harder and therefore more durable. Samuel Roberts, always to the fore with new processes, took out a patent in 1830 whereby silver could be saved by first fusing a sheet of the new nickel alloy to copper, then fusing a thin skin of silver on to that. Since about 1845 nickel silver has been the standard metal used for plating.

Other advantages of the new material, apart from durability, were its adaptability to the process of hard-soldering, and above all its colour: no longer did the plater have to worry about copper showing through in weak places.

It was not long, therefore, before the electro-platers, led by the Elkingtons of Birmingham, overtook the fused platers in providing an acceptable article at far less cost. Nevertheless, even as late as 1851 the judges at the Great Exhibition were still expressing doubts about the new process. Of the electro-plated goods shown there by Elkingtons, they said: 'The Jury desire to guard against being considered as expressing an opinion on the merit of the application of the electro process on silver plating to objects of domestic use. They desire only to commend the artistic application of this process to which alone they are inclined to think it adapted.' On the other hand, they awarded a prize medal to T. J. & N. Creswick for goods 'plated by the old process of uniting metals by heat'. They considered the articles 'important in size and of good taste'. Candelabra of the style of Louis XIV

Tea urns, 1780–1820.

and Louis XV were especially mentioned and the workmanship of dish-covers, trays and teapots was commended as 'carefully executed and adapted for long use'.

But the end was not far away. A few firms lingered on for a year or two, but in the end they, too, disappeared. Strangely enough, few of the distinguished names in fused plating went over to the new process: this was a new industry, and it found its true home in Birmingham rather than Sheffield. 'Brummagem' had won.

6. Reproductions and Fakes

Even the most expert of collectors must at times tread very warily. There are reproductions and there are fakes. The piece may have been made in exactly the same way as in the old days, using fused plate, rubbed-in silver shields, silver mounts and silver threaded edges. By now it may well have acquired the mellowness required of older wares, and must therefore be adjudged by other means—style, workmanship, etc.

Another class of reproduction, mostly from Birmingham, uses dies of the 'Florid' or decadent period and generally shows a lack of good proportions. Some pieces have designs from before the days of silver-threaded edges and mounts and plated wire and are therefore extremely difficult to detect; there may, however, be signs of the tiny holes in the surface which betray them—something alien to the plate makers. There are others, of foreign origin, which have silver threads soft-soldered to electro-plated copper bodies; they even have the words SILVER EDGES stamped on the lids. Wire-work dessert baskets are also popular subjects for reproduction.

There are a number of ways in which the collector can protect himself from these deceptions. One, of course, is to buy only from the specialist dealer, and ask for his written guarantee of the genuineness of the article offered. In this case, one buys the article at the full current market price, and if the piece proves to be bogus, or to fall short in any way of the standard claimed, it can be returned.

The other way is to arm oneself with the equipment of the connoisseur. One has to learn to observe the difference between the actual colour of silver alloy on copper as distinct from that of pure silver on electro-plate: the one has

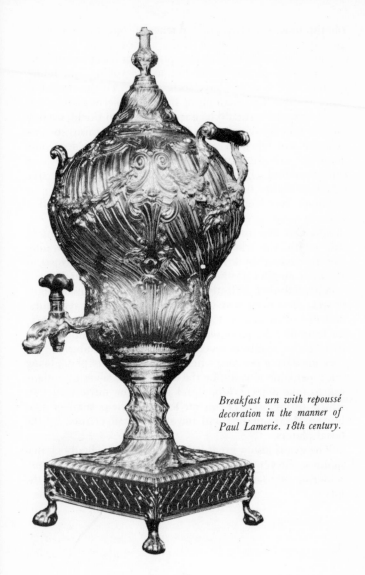

Breakfast urn with repoussé decoration in the manner of Paul Lamerie. 18th century.

a bluish tone, because of the presence of copper in the alloy, the other is a cold, hard white. Fused plate, one also discovers, is harder than electro-plate: this is due not only to the difference in the metal but to the rolling and hammering, which, as we have seen, have given the surface a closer texture. On medium or large size pieces made after about 1789 there should be a rubbed-in silver shield, even if there is no engraving on it. The failure to burnish—necessary for the faker to avoid making the piece look too 'modern'—also tells its tale in a scratchy surface. One will expect to find chasing rather than deep engraving, fly-punching rather than saw-piercing.

Time is very well spent in examining hinges, which, after years of wear, are entitled to a degree of looseness. One should also look on spouts, handles, feet, etc. for signs of seams with faint traces of solder—although these joins may well be covered by a mount. Edges should be inspected to see what method has been used to hide the copper.

A good deal of perfectly genuine plate, after showing signs of wear, has been sent to the electro-platers for replating, and this often makes it extremely difficult to tell whether, for example, the piece was originally plated on one side or two; it also negatives several of the tests given above.

Some daring persons, when offered a piece of plate, bring out a penknife to examine the depth of the silvering: others ask to take a piece home and give it the nitric acid test, which distinguishes chemically between the pure silver used by the electro-platers and the standard silver used by the fused platers.

The eye is also a great help in other ways. Badly chosen mounts, uneven sides due to lack of hammering, clumsy soldering, signs of the file, all help to betray the hand of the faker.

7. Marks on Fused Plate

From the very beginnings the platers tried to make their wares resemble silver as closely as possible. It did no harm—to them at any rate—if the marks on them also looked rather like those on silver. So even the very earliest of the platers—for example Joseph Hancock and Thomas Law—arranged their initials and various symbols in the same style and on the same places as did the silversmiths, sometimes repeating these devices to simulate the stamp of the assay office, the lion and the maker's mark.

This practice continued until 1773, when the silversmiths of Sheffield and Birmingham successfully petitioned Parliament to establish assay offices for silverwork in both towns. They hoped by this move to establish some degree of control over the platers, and also to reduce their own expenses in having to send their wares to London or other provincial offices to be hallmarked. The Act establishing the new Assay Offices also carried a clause prohibiting the striking of any letter, or letters, on goods 'Made of metal, plated or covered with silver, or upon any metal vessel or other thing made to look like silver': the penalty being a fine of £100.

But this was going too far: it meant that the platers could not even use honest marks, and would so be prevented from establishing their reputations as platers. So in 1784 another Act was put on the Statute Book which recognized this fact and permitted the maker to strike his wares with 'his or her surname, or, in the case of any partnership the name of the firm of such partnership, and also some mark, figure, or device, to be struck at the end of such surname, or other name of firm: such mark, figure or device not being the same or in imitation of any mark made use of by any Assay

Office. . . .' The names had to be 'in plain and legible characters and struck with one punch only'.

This meant that while there was not, as in the case of silver, an obligation to mark plated goods, they could be marked only in the approved form as duly registered at the Sheffield Office. The rule extended to platers 'one hundred miles from Sheffield', a measure aimed at the Birmingham platers, who, to their great disgust, had now to register their marks at Sheffield.

Actually, in the early years very few of the platers took the trouble to register their marks. Only five firms in Birmingham and eleven in Sheffield registered at once; and even by the year 1806, there was only one further registration from Birmingham, while Sheffield men had come in at the rate of only one or two a year. From 1807 onwards, in which year there was a sudden flood of registrations from Birmingham, apparently due to the revival of close-plating, the latter town took over the lead until marking died out altogether, the last two names appearing in 1836. From the beginning in 1784, there had been in all eighty registrations from Birmingham, fifty-two from Sheffield and one from London—Stanley and Thomas Howard of St Paul's Churchyard, London, makers of close-plated wares.

Only very few of the Birmingham platers to register, it seems, were makers of the kind of plated goods we have been

Two-handled cups, 18th century.

considering in these pages: they were for the most part manufacturers of buttons, buckles, harness furniture, jewellery and the like, who probably had in any case marked their goods in some way before the passing of the two Acts.

In spite of all these registrations, relatively few pieces of Sheffield plate, whether from Sheffield itself or Birmingham, actually bear marks. Frederick Bradbury thought this was due to the fact that articles intended for the London market—which must have been an enormous consumer —would, when marked at all, most likely bear the mark of the retailer rather than the maker, the latter being naturally anxious to secure the goodwill of profitable outlets: this same practice occurred in the china trade.

The Acts do not seem to have been seriously enforced except in the matter of the imitation silver marks, for we find all kind of nominal irregularities occurring. Sometimes the firm's name was omitted, only the device being used: this was probably due to a desire to make the marking as inconspicuous as possible. Seemingly those who omitted a mark altogether had decided that it was safer to do this than to flout the regulations by using a partial mark.

The most frequently found marks, especially on finely made wares from 1805 onwards, are those of Matthew Boulton & Co., whose device was a sun; they were followed

Hot water jugs, late 18th century.

closely by Roberts, Cadman & Co with their bell. Another mark often encountered is the open hand. This was first registered by Nathaniel Smith in 1784, and often appears in conjunction with his name. In 1810 it was registered again, apparently by a subsequent partnership of the same family, and later on, when the firm was taken over by John Watson & Son, the device was inherited as well. There are even more complex instances than this of the use of a device by different combinations of firms and individuals, and the collector has to pick his way carefully among them if he wishes to establish a date from the mark.

There are quite a few unsolved puzzles. A crown was used by some makers—in spite of this being the official device of the Sheffield Assay Office for silver. It has been suggested that it may have been added by Joseph Rodgers & Sons, the Sheffield factors or wholesalers, who had a Royal Warrant.

About the year 1820 there was another outbreak of imitating silver hallmarks—much more successfully than in the pre-1784 era. Workmen's marks are also to be found, in some cases near the maker's mark and therefore liable to be confused with it. There are also series of stock numbers, and sometimes an indication of capacity.

The fullest account of marking problems on Old Sheffield Plate is to be found in Frederick Bradbury's book on the subject, which remains the standard work.

Vase and cover with copper liner.
Late 18th century.